# DATE DUE

|  |  |
|---|---|
|  |  |
|  |  |
|  |  |
|  |  |
|  |  |
|  |  |
|  |  |
|  |  |
|  |  |
|  |  |
|  |  |
|  |  |
|  |  |
|  |  |
|  |  |
|  |  |
|  |  |

PRINTED IN U.S.A.

# SLIDING

GLOBAL CITIZENS: OLYMPIC SPORTS

Published in the United States of America by Cherry Lake Publishing
Ann Arbor, Michigan
www.cherrylakepublishing.com

Content Adviser: Liv Williams, Editor, www.iLivExtreme.com
Reading Adviser: Marla Conn MS, Ed., Literacy specialist, Read-Ability, Inc.

Photo Credits: ©Daniel Hurlimann / Shutterstock.com, cover, 14, 16, 22; ©ID1974 / Shutterstock.com, 5;
©Aksenova Natalya / Shutterstock.com, 6; ©Photographed by Tim Hipps [2014] / The U.S. Army / flickr.com, 8;
©Iurii Osadchi / Shutterstock.com, 11, 23, 24; ©Photographed by Tim Hipps [2010] / FMWRC Public Affairs /
U.S. Army / flickr.com, 12; ©Dainis Derics / Shutterstock.com, 13; ©Jon Wick / flickr.com, 15, 19, 21;
©Herbert Kratky / Shutterstock.com, 20; ©Kvanta / Shutterstock.com, 27; ©Photographed by Tim Hipps
[2010] / U.S. Army IMCOM / defense.gov, 28; The appearance of U.S. Department of Defense (DoD) visual
information does not imply or constitute DoD endorsement.

Library of Congress Cataloging-in-Publication Data has been filed and is available at catalog.loc.gov

Cherry Lake Publishing would like to acknowledge the work of The Partnership for 21st Century Learning.
Please visit *www.p21.org* for more information.

Printed in the United States of America
Corporate Graphics

## ABOUT THE AUTHOR

Ellen Labrecque has written over 100 books for children. She loves the Olympics and has
attended both the Winter and Summer Games as a reporter for magazines and television.
She lives in Yardley, Pennsylvania, with her husband, Jeff, and her two young "editors,"
Sam and Juliet. When she isn't writing, she is running, hiking, and reading.

# TABLE OF CONTENTS

# History: Sledding to Sliding

The first Winter Olympics was held in Chamonix, France, from January 25 to February 5, 1924. It included 258 athletes from 16 different countries competing in 16 events. Since then, the Winter Olympics has been held every 4 years in a number of countries. (The Games were skipped in 1940 and 1944 during World War II.) As the Games progressed, more competitors and events were added. Fast-forward to the 2014 Winter Games held in Sochi, Russia. There were 2,873 competitors from 88 different countries competing in 98 events. That's a lot more competitors and events!

From the graceful choreography of figure skating to the lightning-speed action in hockey, the Winter Games display some of the most unbelievable sports and athletes. Sliding

The Sliding Center Sanki, which held the 2014 Olympic sliding events, is 5,951 feet (1,814 m) long.

sports—which include bobsledding, luge, and skeleton—are some of the speediest and most daring events in all of the Games.

## The Story of Sledding

Sledding—or sliding down a snow-covered slope or ice shoot—has been a favorite winter activity for both young and old. But sleds, or **toboggans**, weren't always used for fun. At first they were used for work, transporting people and goods across the snow-filled tundra. The first snow sleds were made from birch and were 7 to 10 feet (2 to 3 meters) long but only 1 foot

Sleds were originally used for transporting goods and not for sliding down snowy hills!

(30.5 centimeters) wide. The sleds were made narrow on purpose so they could slide easily on a snowshoe path. Sledding slowly became a sport during the 1800s. Different clubs, like the Montreal Tobogganing Club in Canada, started sponsoring competitions and races.

Today, downhill sledding has transitioned into a more serious Olympic sport. Bobsledding, luge, and skeleton all use the same icy track and fall under the umbrella of sliding. But they each use slightly different kinds of sleds and techniques. In bobsledding, teams of two or four athletes compete by sitting and steering a sled down the track. The bobsled includes seats, a device that allows the driver to steer left and right, and a brake that the brakeman controls. Luge has either one person lying on a sled (in singles) or two people lying on top of each other (in doubles) racing down the icy slope. Skeleton has one person lying face down on a flat sled going headfirst! Lugers and bobsledders reach speeds of over 90 miles (145 kilometers) per hour, while skeleton racers reach speeds of over 80 mph (129 kph)!

## Welcome to the Olympics

Bobsledding—also known as bobsleighing—was invented in the late 1800s by attaching two sleds together. *Bob* was added to the word *sled* because at first people tried to bob their head in different directions to steer. Today, the bobsled driver steers by pulling on cords that are attached to the **runners** at the bottom of the sled. The driver sits at the front of the sled and the brakeman sits at the back. The other two athletes (in a four-person team) keep their heads down the entire time. The four-person race was an event at the first Winter Olympics in 1924. The two-person competition was added in 1932. The women's two-person team did not start competing in the Olympics until 2002.

These luge athletes were clocked going 80 mph (128.7 kph)!

Luge is considered the most dangerous of the three sliding sports because it is the fastest with the least protection. It is also the only one where the athlete starts out on the sled. In the other sports, the athletes jump in after the sled starts moving. In luge, racers lie down feetfirst and pull themselves forward by pushing off on a pair of rods. Men's and women's singles luge was first included in the Olympics in 1964. Men's doubles was also included that same year. After the 1992 Olympics, both men and women were allowed to compete in the doubles event.

Men's skeleton was first included in the Winter Olympics in 1928. Then it took a break until 1948, when it appeared again at the Games. It took one more break after that and didn't return to the Winter Olympics until 2002, during which the women's events were added. Skeleton racers slide down the mountain headfirst. They don't fly quite as fast as lugers, but they are still going faster than a car on a highway!

## Developing Claims and Using Evidence

Lugers fly down the hill faster than skeleton racers. Part of the reason is because skeleton racers go headfirst and wear a big, round helmet. Lugers wear helmets, too, but their head is at the back of the sled, not the front. Why might sliding down headfirst with a helmet on slow down a racer?

# CHAPTER 2

# Geography: The World's Best Sliders

At the 2014 Winter Olympics, 326 athletes participated in bobsled, luge, and skeleton. There were a total of 169 bobsledders from 23 nations, 110 lugers from 24 nations, and 47 skeleton racers from 17 nations competing. Which countries have won the most Olympic medals in these sliding sports?

The German two-person bobsled team came in eighth place during the 2014 Games.

## Bobsled

Germany is the king of Olympic bobsledding. Despite not winning a medal in 2014, Germans have won at least one medal in every Olympics since 1968, for a total of 40 medals. Switzerland has won 31 men's bobsledding medals. The United States has dominated more recently, winning four bobsledding medals at the 2014 Games in both the men's and women's teams, the most of any country during that Olympic season.

Athletes must be perfect in their technique in order to avoid accidents.

Luge athletes use sleds that are specially designed with steel blades that curve up to support their legs.

## Luge

Germany also dominates the luge tracks. Since 1980, Germany has won more than half (58 percent) of all luge medals, including a sweep at the 2014 Games. Out of the total 129 Olympic medals for men's, women's, and team relay, Germany has won 75. Thirty-one of those 75 medals are gold. Italy comes in at a far second place with a total of 17 medals, seven of which are gold. That's a big difference!

To brake, luge athletes pull on the front of their sled while digging their feet into the course.

Everyone wants to know the secret to Germany's success. One reason might be the **technical** aspect of the sledding. Germans are always thinking of ways to redesign their sled to shave off tenths of seconds on their run. Germany also has the most luge tracks compared to any other country. There are a total of 16 luge tracks around the world. Four are located in Germany. Other countries have maybe one or two. Another reason the country may have the advantage is because German kids grow up learning the sport. Many schools even have luge programs. Everybody there wants to be a luger!

A luge athlete at the start of a run.

Skeleton racers sprint forward on the course before diving headfirst onto their sled.

## Skeleton

Skeleton hasn't been a part of many Olympics, but the United States has won the most medals (eight total, including three gold) in the years it has been included. Great Britain has also been strong in skeleton, winning six medals in total, including two gold. It is the only team that has won a skeleton medal in every Olympics that the sport has been included.

## Gathering and Evaluating Sources

There are only 16 bobsledding tracks around the world. The United States has only two tracks in the entire country. Four of the seven continents do not have tracks at all. Using the Internet and your local library, list the continents with and without the tracks. Compare this list to the top competitors in bobsledding. Do countries with more bobsledding tracks perform better than countries with very few or none at all? Why or why not? Use the data you find to support your answer.

# Civics: Olympic Pride

Hosting the Olympic Games can be a big source of pride for the city and the people who live there. It gives the citizens a chance to show off where they live to the entire world. Also, the athletes and fans who come to the Games spend a lot of money there. One of the biggest ways the host country shows off is at the opening and closing ceremonies. More than 3 billion people watched the opening of the 2014 Winter Games in Sochi, Russia! Olympic hosts set up cameras all over the track so fans can watch every second of their favorite bobsled, luge, and skeleton teams and athletes zipping down the icy shoot.

At the 2010 Games, Amy Williams, a skeleton racer, became the first British woman to win gold in an individual event since the 1952 Games.

Host cities go through a rigorous process before even being considered a candidate for the Games.

A skeleton athlete prepares for the race.

## Small but Popular

Fans want to watch athletes from their country win. Great Britain and Germany are no different. When Lizzy Yarnold of Great Britain won the gold medal in skeleton at the 2014 Games, 4.7 million people from her home country watched her do it. This was the biggest audience to watch any Winter Olympic sporting event there since 2002.

German fans—9.2 million of them, to be exact—tuned in to watch Felix Loch win his second straight gold medal in men's

To date, Felix Loch of Germany is the youngest gold medalist in Olympic men's luge.

At the 1994 Games, the Jamaican four-person bobsled team surprised everyone by placing ahead of several countries, including the United States, France, and Sweden.

luge. (He won the gold in 2010, too.) This was the most watched Winter Olympic event in Germany during the 2014 Games.

Even though many people love to watch the sliding sports in the Olympics, only a small number of people are skilled enough to compete. In fact, Germany, which loves its sliding sports, has only 8,000 members in the luge federation and fewer than 10,000 members in the bobsledding and skeleton federation. In contrast, there are 650,000 members in Germany's skiing federation, 81 times more than luge!

Fans from all over the world were cheering on the "Hottest Thing on Ice."

## "Hottest Thing on Ice"

Athletes from cold countries usually compete in the Winter Olympics. But Jamaica, a country in the Caribbean Sea where the average temperature is 80 degrees Fahrenheit (27 degrees Celsius) year-round, had one of the most famous bobsledding teams of all time. The Jamaican team competed at the 1988 Games in Calgary, Canada. Leading up to the Games, the team practiced in Austria. Although the team didn't come close to winning a medal, it filled its tiny island nation with pride. A movie, *Cool Runnings*, was based on this Jamaican team. It made almost $155 million around the world. The team was nicknamed the "Hottest Thing on Ice." A Jamaican team competed again most recently at the 2014 Games. While it finished in last place, that didn't stop its spirit, as the team plans on competing in the 2018 Games.

## Developing Claims

*Watch the movie* Cool Runnings *about the Jamaican bobsledding team. Go online and read about the true story of the team. How were parts of the movie the same? How were they different? Is it okay that some parts of the movie weren't entirely true? Why or why not?*

# CHAPTER 4

# Economics: Sliding Is Big Business

Hosting the Olympic Games costs a lot of money. PyeongChang, South Korea, the host of the 2018 Winter Olympics, has spent $114.5 million just on the Alpensia Sliding Center for the Games! This doesn't include the cost of any of the other **venues**—even the stadium for the opening and closing ceremonies. The city hopes to earn back a lot of that money once the Olympics begins.

## The Fans

**Tourists** come to the city to see the Olympics. They spend money by staying in hotels, buying souvenirs, and eating in the city's restaurants. The sliding center at the 2018 Games will allow 7,000 fans to watch the sliding events. Each ticket, depending on the event, will cost anywhere from $150 to $400.

Tickets for the opening and closing ceremonies at the
2018 Games cost $192 to $1,310!

The women's bobsled team were outfitted by Under Armour during the 2010 Games.

## Taking Informed Action

*Do you want to learn more about the Winter Olympics and the sliding sports (bobsled, luge, and skeleton)? There are many different organizations that you can explore. Check them out online. Here are three to start your search:*

- *Team USA—Bobsled & Skeleton: Learn more about the US Bobsled and Skeleton Teams on the official website.*

- *Team USA—Luge: Read more about the US Luge Team on the official website.*

- *NBC Olympics: Find out all you can about the upcoming 2018 Winter Olympic Games in PyeongChang, South Korea.*

## The Sponsors

Advertisers like Coca-Cola and McDonald's pay a lot of money to sponsor the Olympics. Their signs and logos appear in television commercials and on boards all over the venues. Sponsor logos also appear on the actual bobsleds, on the athletes' helmets, and on the luge and skeleton sleds. Under Armour, an athletic clothing company, makes all the skeleton, bobsledding, and luge team uniforms for the United States and Canada. During the 2014 games, Under Armour ran a commercial that included US bobsledders who were battling freezing temperatures but were protected by the company's gear!

## Communicating Conclusions

Before reading this book, did you know much about the sliding events and the Winter Olympics? Now that you know more, do you think more people in the United States should watch this sport? Do you think more tracks should be built around the world so more kids can participate? Share what you learned about the sport with friends at school or with your family.

# Think About It

Since its Olympic debut in 1964, luge has held three events: singles, mixed team relay, and doubles. Men competed in all three events. Women were only allowed to compete in the singles and mixed team relay. It wasn't until after the 1992 Games that women were included in the doubles event. However, in the first 25 years of the luge doubles event being open to women, there has yet to be a single woman who has competed! Why do you think this is? Use the data you find to support your argument.

# For More Information

## Further Reading

Johnson, Robin. *Bobsleigh, Luge, and Skeleton*. New York: Crabtree Publishing, 2010.

Wallechinsky, David, and Jaime Loucky. *The Complete Book of the Winter Olympics*. Hertford, NC: Crossroad Press, 2014.

Waxman, Laura Hamilton. *Bobsled and Luge*. Mankato, MN: Amicus Ink, 2018.

## Websites

**The International Olympic Committee**
https://www.olympic.org/the-ioc
Discover how the IOC works to build a better world through sports.

**International Bobsleigh and Skeleton Federation**
www.ibsf.org/en
Find great maps of the world's bobsledding tracks.

# GLOSSARY

**runners** (RUHN-erz) thin pieces or parts on the bottom of a sled that help it slide

**technical** (TEK-nih-kuhl) skill that is difficult to master

**toboggans** (tuh-BOG-uhnz) long, narrow, flat-bottomed sleds

**tourists** (TOOR-ists) people who are traveling for pleasure

**venues** (VEN-yooz) places where actions or events occur

# INDEX